Who's Munching My Milkweed?

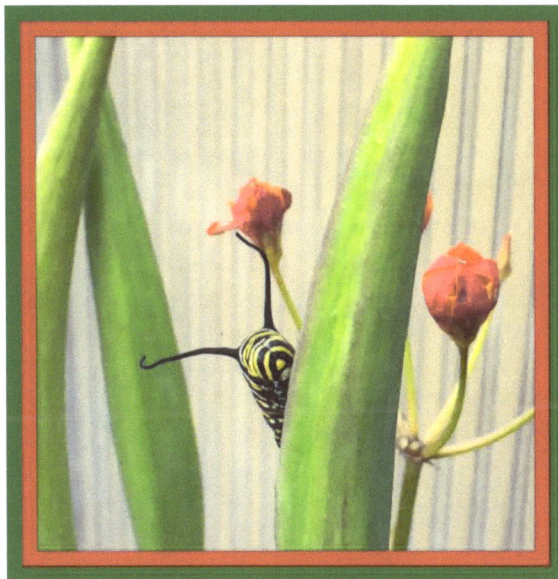

by

Smoky Zeidel

For even more information, activities, and recipes you can follow Sweet Maple and Karate Kid Kale in the book *Sweet! Activity Book*. There, you can practice all the delicious information you learned in this book. See you there!

Who's Munching My Milkweed?

Copyright 2018 by Smoky Zeidel

Milkweed plant on cover: Available from SwallowTailGardenSeeds on Flicker.com under a Creative Commons 2.0 Attribution License. First came from Asclepias tuberosa L. Paxton's Magazine of botany and register of flowering plants vol. 2 (1836). Has been slightly modified for content and texture.

Library of Congress Control Number: 2018941310
1. Juvenile fiction nature and the natural world 2. Juvenile fiction education 3. Juvenile fiction animals/insects, etc.
ISBN 10: 0-9979517-5-3
ISBN-13: 978-0-9979517-5-2
Thomas-Jacob Publishing, LLC, Deltona, Florida USA
Contact the publisher at TJPub@thomas-jacobpublishing.com.

Thomas-Jacob Publishing, LLC
USA

Dedication

For the bugs, the bees, and the butterflies.
But most of all, for the caterpillars.

"Who's munching my milkweed?" Ms. Gardener said.
"Just look at these chewed leaves! They hang by a thread!"

Then she looked closer,
and saw quite a sight,

Caterpillars striped
in black, yellow, and white!

"Monarchs!" she said as she dropped to her knees.
"Sharing the milkweed with bugs and with bees!"

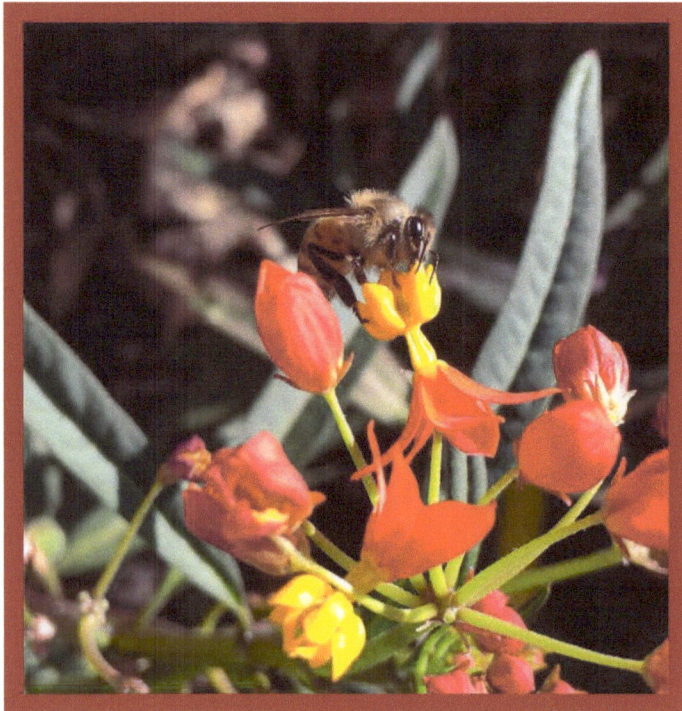

"And there is an egg, so soon
there'll be another!

Good grief!

Does this make me a monarch
grandmother?"

The caterpillars all were quite different in size,

With six pairs of true legs
and six pairs of eyes.

Another ten prolegs
(false legs you might hear),

And two sets of tentacles,
one front and one rear.

"Fifteen caterpillars," she said, counting fast.
Then she frowned. She was worried. Would the milkweed last?
"They'll eat only milkweed, that much I do know.
If they run out of milkweed, just where will they go?"

She counted her milkweed plants.
There were five.

Would that be enough
to keep them alive?

Each day she watched the caterpillars devour
the milkweed plants—leaf, seed pod, and flower.
When one plant was bare, they moved onto another.
Oh, what will I do?" moaned the monarch grandmother.
There's only four plants, not many to go.
Please don't eat so fast!

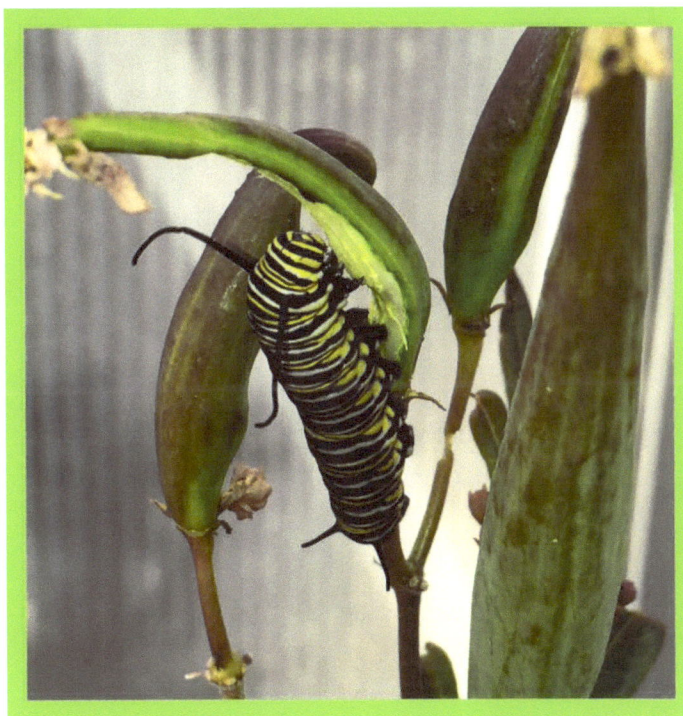

Why can't you eat slow?"

A mockingbird sang from the top of the tree
she heard its sweet song and the hum of a bee.
The number of milkweed plants now was just three.

Ms. Gardener sat down
to watch the cats eat.

Munch munch, went the cats
while the bird sang *tweet tweet.*

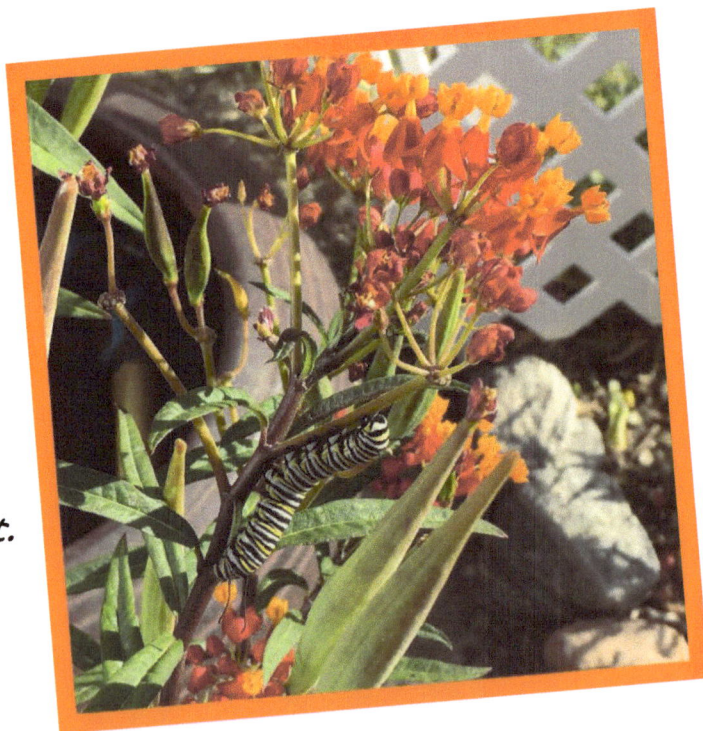

Then tragedy struck! The bird grabbed from a leaf
a plump caterpillar ... that mockingbird thief!

"Drop that cat!" roared Ms. Gardener. "You drop it now, quick!
Don't you know they are poisonous? You'll make yourself sick!"

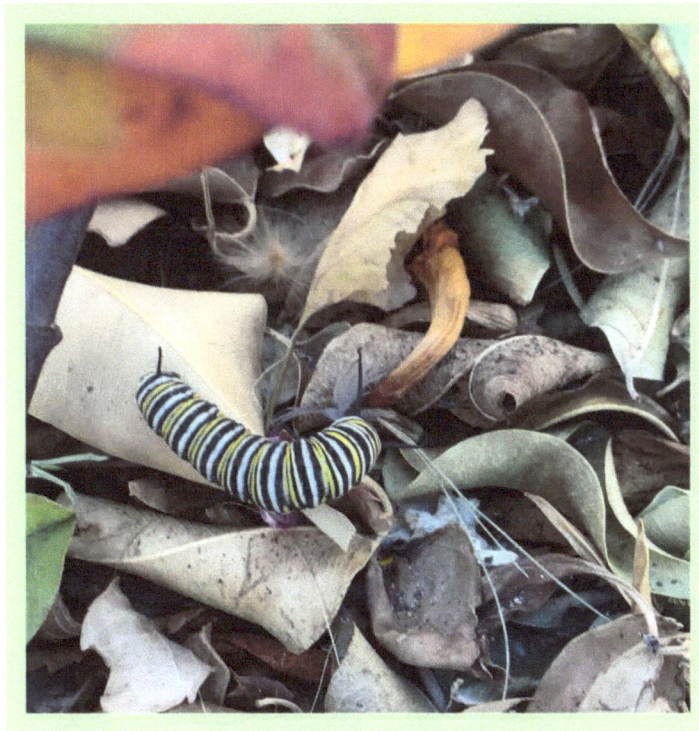

With a flutter and squawk and a sick gagging sound
the bird dropped the caterpillar down on the ground.

She cradled the cat in the palm of her hand,
and gently brushed off a few grains of sand.

Then lo and behold,
to Ms. Gardener's delight

the caterpillar recovered
from its awful fright!

After playing dead for a moment so brief,
it crawled off her hand and back onto a leaf.

The caterpillars grew so much bigger each day!
They munched through the milkweed like horses through hay.

When they grew too much,
their skin became tight,

so they crawled right out of
it—now that was a sight!

"You've molted, I see," Ms. Gardener said
as the the cats turned and munched the skin they had shed.

After more than a week the plants numbered just two,
Ms. Gardener said, "I don't know what I should do!

Fifteen cats on two
plants,

how will they survive?

I don't know how I will keep them alive!"

Two more days passed and now the plants were just one!
Filled with huge caterpillars! She said, "Aren't you done?

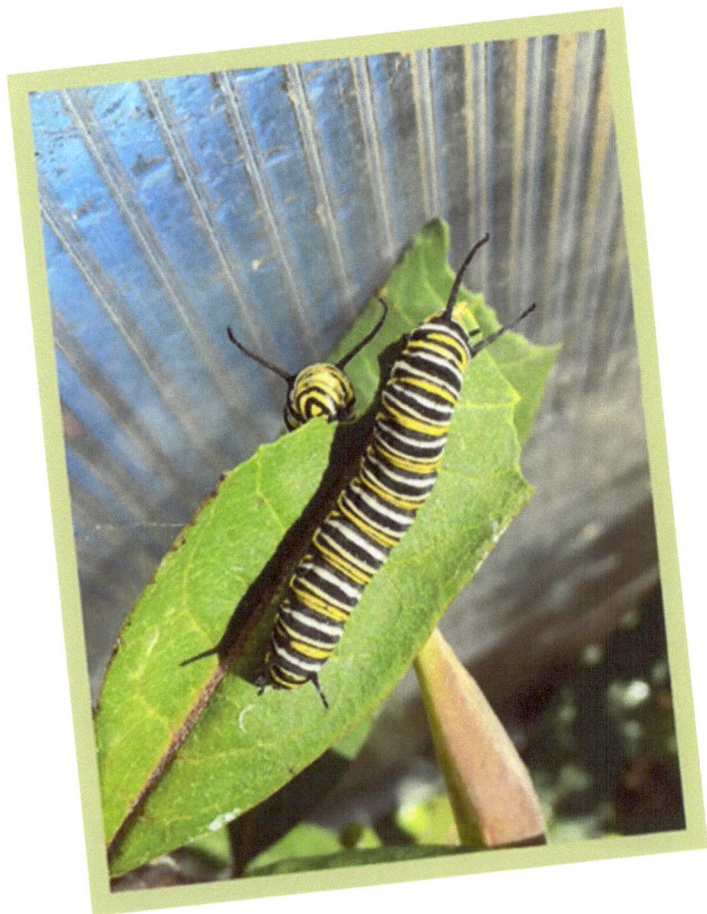

There's almost no milkweed,
almost nothing to eat!

Don't you think that it's time
you all hit the street?"

Then a miracle happened! They all seemed to listen!
They crawled off the milkweed as if on a mission.

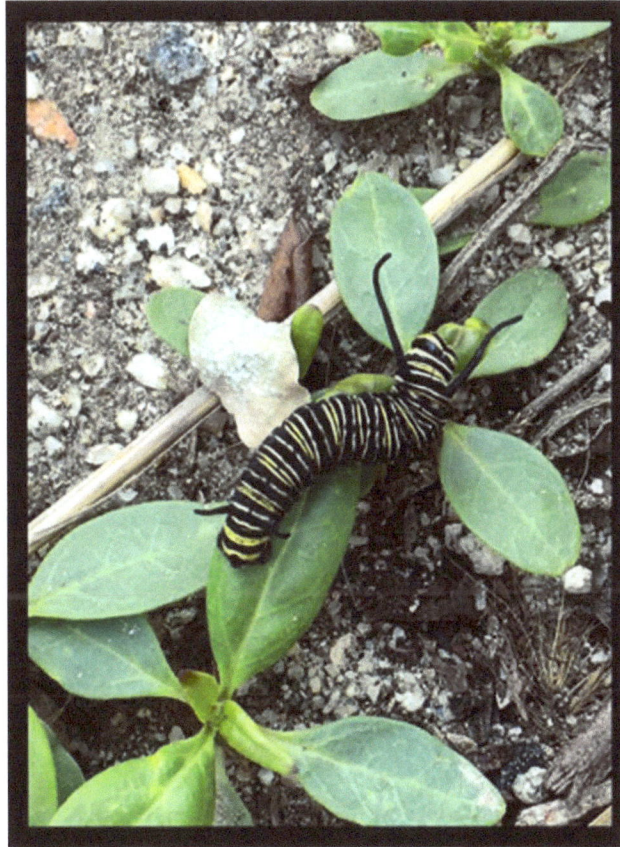

Some traveled so far they went to the next yard
She bid them *adieu*. Saying goodbye hard!

One crawled up the cloth that gave the plants shade,

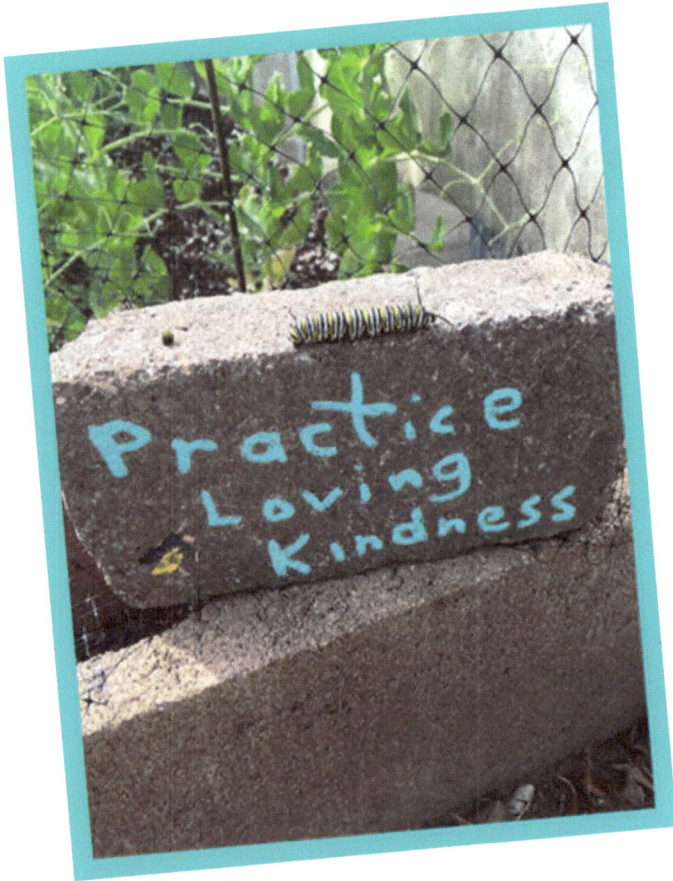

One crawled up the rock wall a neighbor had made.

One climbed up the back fence of twisted gray wire,

They each found a spot, some down low, some up higher.

They hung like a "J" from a spun silken thread,
They hung there for hours, as if they were dead.

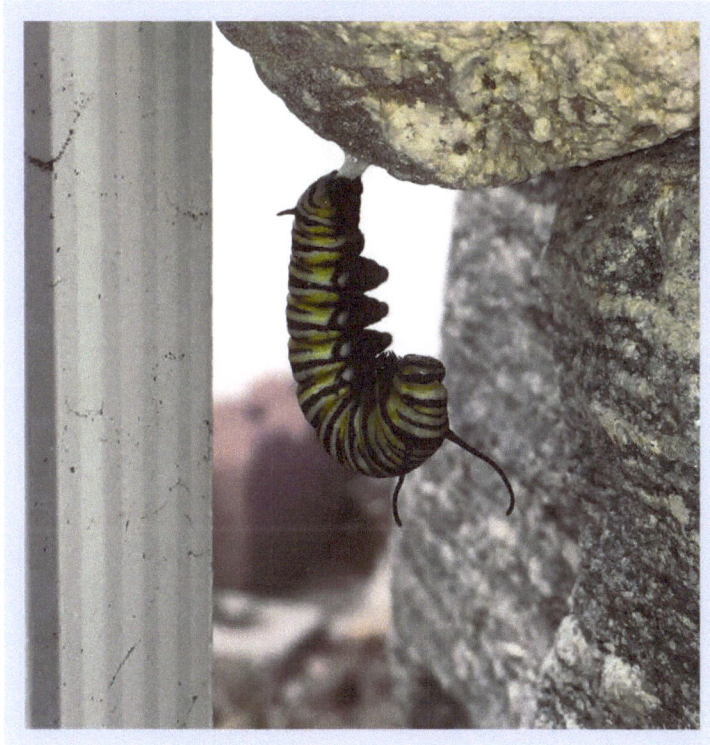

But Ms. Gardener knew better, knew soon each would change,
Each would become a chrysalis, wondrous and strange.

She watched as a cat wiggled out of its skin,
and became a green pupa. She said with a grin,

"It's almost as if you are
now inside out!

So this is what pupating
is all about!"

Said Ms. Gardener, "I've never seen magic like this,
A caterpillar becoming a green chrysalis!"

She watched and she waited, she tended her yard,
She planted tomatoes and green beans and chard.

She cut back the milkweed and watched it resprout.

Soon it would look like she'd never run out!

Then one day a chrysalis no longer was green.

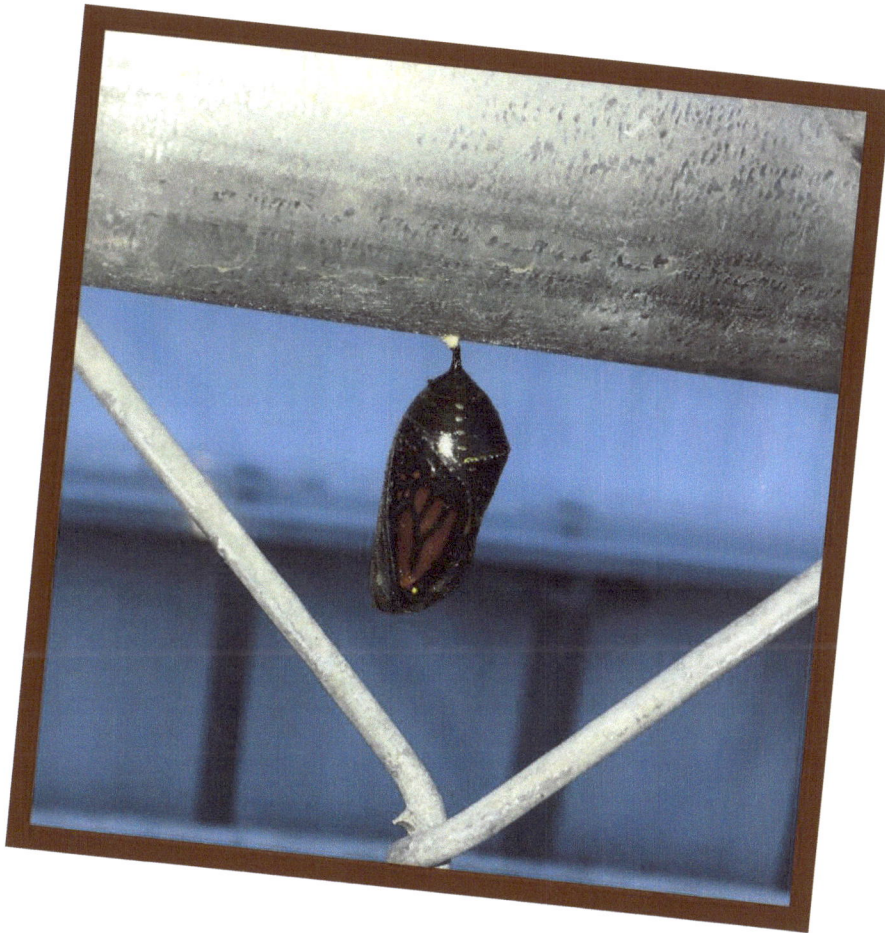

Inside the clear casing a monarch was seen.

Soon it hatched, or eclosed, as the scientists say,
Ms. Gardener exclaimed, "Now that just makes my day!

A new monarch butterfly now
will fly free!

A more beautiful sight I never did see!"

She held out her hand and remaining quite calm,
the butterfly stepped on Ms. Gardener's palm.

It stayed several minutes, much to her surprise,

then it fluttered its wings and took to the skies.

By the following day more monarchs did hatch,

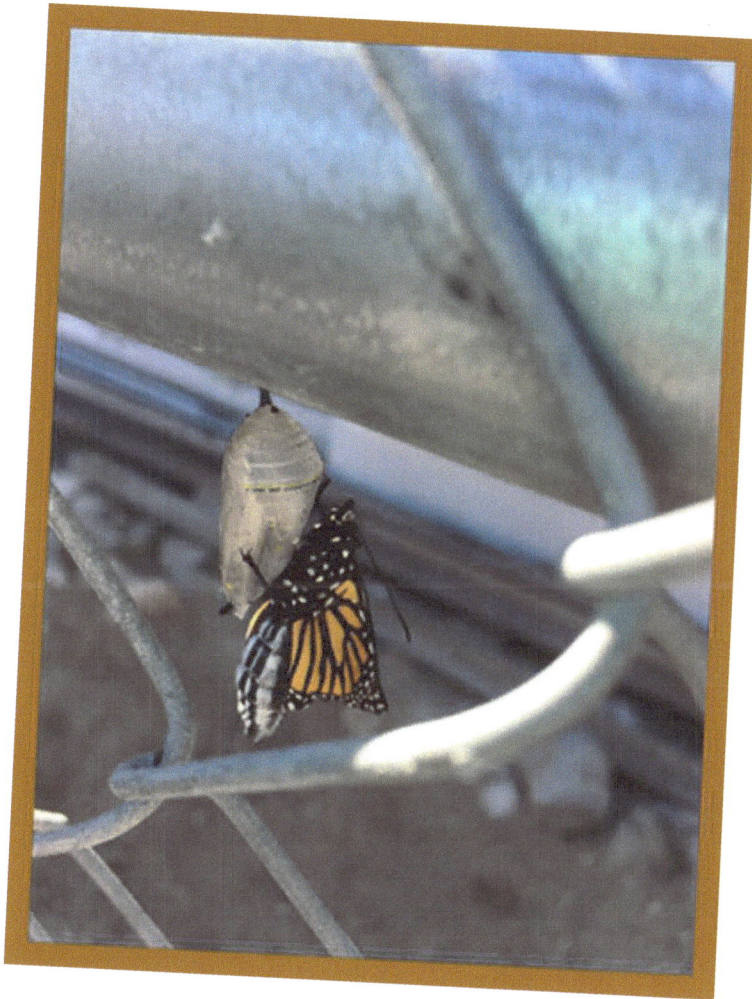

in the trees and the rocks
and the old thistle patch.

"They sure hid themselves well," Ms. Gardener did say.
"But no matter—they're here now this fine warm spring day!"

Fifteen monarch butterflies where once there were none
in her yard, in her garden. She said, "It's been fun!

"I love you," she whispered as they all flew away,
"I hope you'll come back and see me some day."

Soon milkweed had grown back and flowered once more.

New milkweed plants carpeted her garden floor.

Then one day Ms. Gardener happened to spot,
On the leaf of a milkweed a tiny white dot!

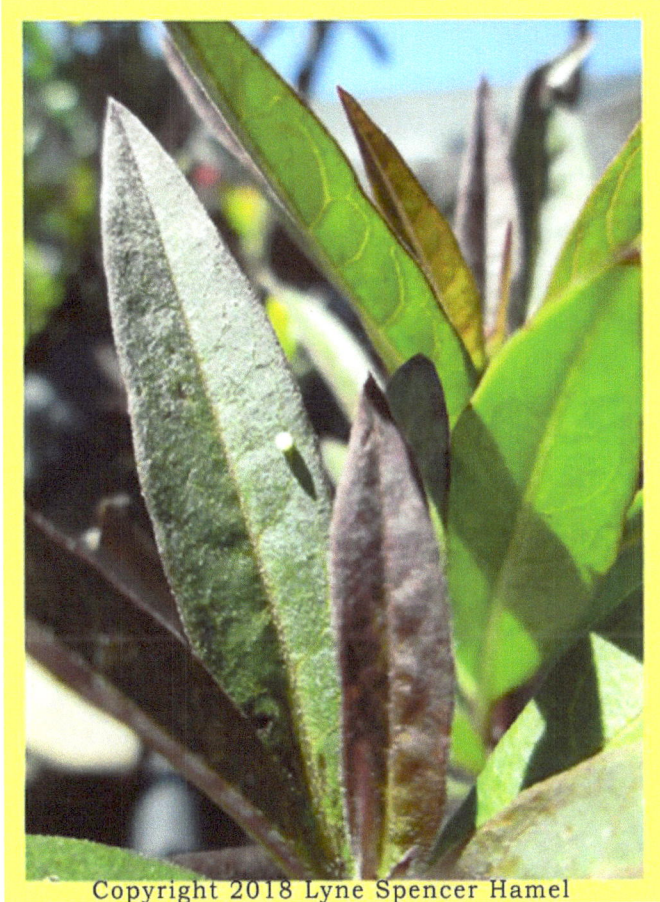

And another, and more!

Monarch eggs, there were ten!

Ms. Gardener cried, "Oh joy, here we go again!"

The End

Tropical milkweed, before and after monarch caterpillars

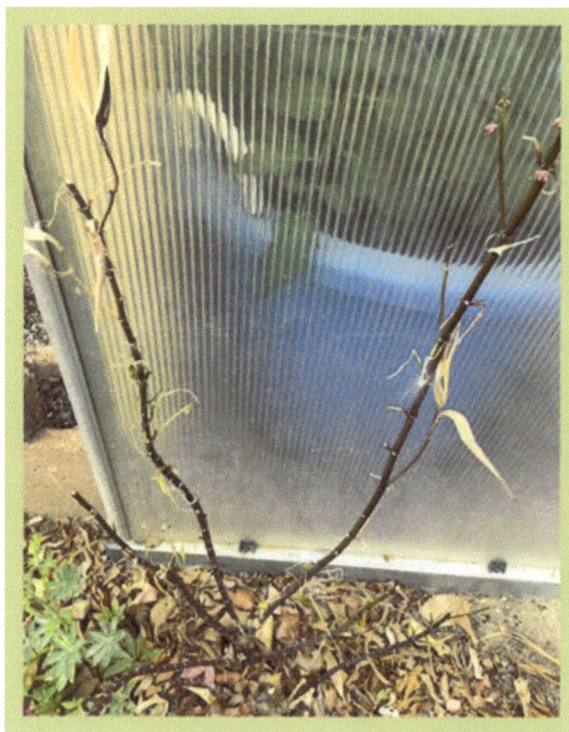

Fun Facts About Monarch Caterpillars

Monarch butterflies go through four different stages in life: **egg**, **larva** (**caterpillar**), **pupa** (**chrysalis**), and **adult**.

Monarch caterpillars shed their skin five times as they grow! This is called **molting**. Each stage of development between moltings is called an **instar**. The caterpillars often eat their shed skin as it is a good source of protein.

The fifth instar caterpillars **pupate**. This is when the caterpillar becomes a **chrysalis**.

Ten days or so (depending on the temperature) after the caterpillar pupates, a new monarch butterfly hatches, or **ecloses**. A new monarch butterfly now flies free.

A female monarch butterfly can mate and lay eggs when she is just four days old. Monarchs lay eggs only on milkweed plants, because that is the only food monarch caterpillars eat. Can you imagine being only able to eat one type of food, like lettuce?

Milkweed is poisonous! When monarch caterpillars eat the milkweed, they become poisonous too. Birds, lizards, and other predators learn very quickly that eating a monarch caterpillar will make them sick. But that doesn't mean they don't sometimes try, like the mockingbird in our story.

You can raise monarch caterpillars too! There are different types of milkweed, and one kind or another grows just about everywhere in North America. If you plant milkweed in your yard, monarch butterflies will find it, and soon you have caterpillars to watch!

About the Author

Smoky Zeidel is a poet and novelist, whose love of the natural world is thematic in all she writes. She taught writing and creativity workshops for many years at venues throughout the Midwest before succumbing to her bohemian urges and moving to Southern California. Her work has earned her five nominations for the prestigious Pushcart Prize.

Smoky lives in the Coachella Valley, which is part of the vast Colorado Desert in Southern California, with her husband Scott, two cats, and a Chihuahua named Tufa (who considers herself the Boss of Everything). She is an avid desert gardener, monarch caterpillar rancher and butterfly midwife.

www.ingramcontent.com/pod-product-compliance
Lightning Source LLC
Chambersburg PA
CBHW060853270326
41934CB00002B/127

9780997951752